The Color of Shadows

"Time flies over us but leaves its shadow behind"

Nathaniel Hawthorne

The Color of Shadows

Carol Townsend

Buffalo Arts Publishing

The Color of Shadows. Copyright © 2019 by Carol Townsend. Printed in the United States of America. All rights reserved. No part of this book may be reproduced or transmitted in any form or by any means without written permission of the author. For information, address Buffalo Arts Publishing, 179 Greenfield Drive, Tonawanda, NY 14150

Email: info@buffaloartspublishing.com

Cover and section photographs by Carol Townsend
Carol Townsend portrait, p. 104, by Nick Butler

ISBN 978-1-950006-06-9
Library of Congress Control Number: 2019947552

Just as the color temperature of shadows changes according to latitude, time of day or year, so too the poems of Townsend's first full-length collection mirror life's experiences. She invites us to share these ephemeral traces—quirky, sexy, tragic and darkly humorous in turn, which are often filtered through the lens of nature.

Acknowledgements

The following poems have appeared in the publications listed below:

"Passage" in *The Sow's Ear Poetry Review*

    "Deceit"
  "The Visit"
"This Ache" in *The Buffalo News*

For John R. Cofield, Jr.

Contents

Ars Poetica

A Poet's Question	15
A Poet's Prayer	16
Poetry Workshop	17
Dissecting *Musee des Beaux Arts*	18
Hunger	19
Polishing	20
Mullein	21
To the Highest Bidder	22
Posture	24
Where the Poem Hides	25
Nest	26
Revenge	27
Among the Palms	28
Color Theory	29
Poets of a Certain Age Meet at Sara's	30
Winter Light	31

Where the Weasel Lurks

Shadowless Days	35
February 13th	36
Anthophobia	37
Garden in Early Morning Light	38
Trowel	39
Perfection	40
Erythrophobia	41
Morning Show	42
Cognitive Dissonance	43
At Thirty-Seven Hundred Feet	44
Cannibal	45

Key Lime Pie 46
Here Among Home 47
Full Buck Moon 49

Stranger than Fiction

Deceit 53
Song of the Perseids 54
Boa Constrictor 55
Reflection in Three Parts 56
Cafe Expose 58
Shostakovich and Outer Space 60
Pluto 61
Concert in the Garden 62
A Crack 63
Lemon and Egg 65
Sciophobia Sciaphobia 66
Ashokin Farewell 67
Still Life in Egg Tempera 68
Bridge 70
Nineteen Men 72
Rozsypne 74
Maple Springs 75
What Remains 76
Compost 77

A Flickering

A Matter of Perspective 81
Five A.M. 82
Every Friday During Lent 83
A Bag of Cloth 84
Regret 85
Agnes Agnes 86
Self-Portrait As One Third Acre 87

Suppose 88
Cobblestones 89
The Calling 90
Annual Visit to Evergreen Cemetery 91
The Night My Sister's House Burned Down 92
Passage 93
The Visit 94

The Yearning

Bluestem 97
Petrichor 98
Unrequited Love 99
Round 100
Passion 101

Special Thanks 103
About the Poet 104

Ars Poetica

A Poet's Questions

Between the desire and the art
   falls the shadow, it is said.

Is that why my poem drags
   in space, not even a tiny speck

of dust in the comet tails
   of Ezra, Robert, Emily?

Why it's just a dirty, dripping
   ice ball of words and images

well outside the solar system?
   A black hole of blah?

So what does this poem need?
   Words that do not wobble?

Music that means?
   Being more than what it says?

I could try sitting at the feet
   of the universe, or, better yet,
      invite *the devil to show up?*

A Poet's Prayer

Let me put aside thin confections,
humorous asides, baffling observations.

Let me cease to be trapped within
the narrow confines of *me*.

Let me inhabit the skins of Emily, Ann,
Susan and Phil, even if I must endure loss.

Let me master the art of attention
and choose the best of the best words.

Better yet, let me learn to slip in the knife
and then, twist it. *Just a little.*

Poetry Workshop

The morning is crowded
with consonant clusters

of st, sl, fl and gl
and liquid vowels

rolling off tongues,
scratching against plosives

in rhythmic complements
of anapest and spondee.

Did I mention alliteration?
Rhyme and limerick?

The ABBA of chiasmus,
and zeugma's yoke?

Now, here's a volta,
the use of caesura…

Dissecting Musee des Beaux Arts

The instructor leans forward,
her eyes bulge, show whites.
Fingers splay as she urges,
"Put a little pressure on the plough.
Use whatever works."

Her gravely voice is a shot
of scotch at eight-thirty A.M.
She is wearing the same dress
and it is damp, rumpled.
A lens has fallen out of her glasses.

The overhead air conditioner
drips into a metal wastebasket.
She grins and says,
"R's and l's are the ball bearings of a line."

Dee's arms are folded.
Holly is definitely in the thrall.
Phyllis squirms, wants a bathroom break.
Maryann moves delicately out
of a strong sunlight beam.

I hold a cup of coffee, wish
the instructor drank less espresso.
She fires up her laser perception--
the target this time is the subtle
rhyme in Auden's poem.

And for a moment, I wish to join Icarus,
a pair of white legs disappearing
into Breughel's green pigmented pond.

Hunger
Fingers in the porridge

My arms are plunged into words
up to the elbows; sarcasm sticks
to my palms. I savor the phrase,
ignore an adjective caught
like a piece of spinach
between my two front teeth.
My cheeks bulge with adverbs.
Clarity puckers my lips
as I gorge on allusion
and *watch for bears.*

Polishing

Some say that water is to rock
what the poet is to words,

but the job demands stink
like paste wax.

Sometimes, a dab of lemon-scented
soap brings out the grain.

Other times, I rub down
to a brassy glow

only to see the shadow
of myself.

Mullein

Between patio bricks,
the soft gray-green rosettes

of verbascum thapsus sprout;
a spike shoots, spiraled

by yellow, star-like flowers.
I leave only one.

My poems lie fallow
in paper shells,

tucked into crevices.
They germinate.

I cultivate.
A single word survives.

To the Highest Bidder

In the living room, I spot the writing desk,
>#214, its surface obscured
>by fluted trays filled with tangles
>of costume jewelry--

not too large, not too fancy. I touch the patina
>left by another woman's hands,
>run my her fingers over curved legs,
>open drawers, note solid wood construction,

envision it placed under the bedroom window
>that looks out over oaks in Amherst,
>New York, and like Emily, will poems flow?
>I want this desk.

Across the room, through opened closet doors,
>silk and satin ball gowns, size four, flare
>their sherbet plumes along with men's suits,
>shoulders thick with dust.

$126 dollars pilfered from all my hiding spots
>burn in my pocket. Wet circles expand under
>my arms. I try to ignore the auction junkies
>who loudly regale each other with tales

of past coups. *#214. Do I hear $200?*
>I nearly stop breathing. A long pause.
>*Do I hear $100?* My hand freezes to the paddle.
>Silence. *Do I hear $50?*

My arm shoots up, exposing its growing penumbra
>of moisture. *Do I hear $75?*
>Up goes my hand. *Sold to number forty-one.*
>I had bid against myself!

With the desk loaded into my van, I notice a man,
    not bidding. "Are you the son?" I ask. He nods.
    His eyes well as I touch his arm. And I tear up, too,
    because years from now, a stranger will note

my own passing, an artistic, eccentric woman
    whose closets bulge with dresses and bangles,
    that stranger whose vehicle holds the writing desk
    from under the window. Not too fancy, not too large.

Posture

The pianist hunches, elbows akimbo,
his shoulders forward under the rise

and fall of full frontal attack.
Now, he half-stands at the bench,

settles back, caresses the keyboard.
Listeners perch on the edge

of benches and Rachmaninoff
himself sits upright, or maybe,

turns over, in his grave.
If only I could collect this electricity,

pour it into a jar over a jumble of syllables,
shake well, marinate for a month.

I would add a few punctuation marks,
stir in tension and action,

a few metaphors.
Fish out abstractions and allegories.

Dead poets and live ones, too,
would pay attention to my words,

ladled out across the page
in complete and perfect form.

At my desk, I realign my spine,
suck in my belly, pick up a pen,
and begin, again.

Where the Poem Hides

My left leg goes everywhere with me,
forgotten, until my mustached muse
slathers it with honey from his hands.

He notes a tracery of fine lines along the arch
where a tendon tore, where heel was sawed,
where steel pin broke behind its threads.

At the calf, he fingers a divot,
a crater formed when the boil broke
during eight grade math.

There are still cinder shadows embedded
in flesh, my knees second rate
to Cousin Marcia's, the Hanes model.

He circles my thigh, an inch less round
than the other, nerve laden with nodes
that steal a career in, say, ballet.

My dimpled derriere, which I was taught
to downplay, quivers where he touches it--
boyfriends past and he must crave cellulite.

This is where he and I found the poem today.
I wonder where it will be tomorrow.
Stuffed into my brassiere?

Nest

Like a sparrow gathers
grasses and threads for her nest,

a safe basket for her brood,
I collect scraps of thought

on strips of paper,
that one day will be wound

into poems, strong vessels
to contain my life.

Revenge
After Frank O'Hara

when I was a child
I wore thick glasses
and hand-me-downs
raised my hand in class

if anyone made me
laugh over lunch
milk would pour
out from my nose

once I read an entire
novel hunched
over an older student's
indifferent shoulder

no one ever picked
me for their team
but no one could imitate
cat sounds better

me, a solitary child
on playground's edge
lurching down the hot
metal slide

and here I am
recording all this
for posterity.
Imagine!

Among the Palms
Buffalo and Erie Country Botanical Gardens

Underneath whitewash clouding
panes too numerous to count,

we poets breathe deeply.
Orchids splendid in ruffled gowns

arch, watch over our shoulders
as shadows become scribbles

coalescing into poems--
we swing from straps of ivy,

nap on plump pillows of moss,
dust with mop-headed mums

and as surely as prickly pear pricks,
we cross-pollinate and grow

ourselves anew in shades of green,
a variegated garden.

Color Theory
Homage to Frank Law Olmstead's Delaware Park

On this day of slate in Buffalo, New York,
a single-file of poets takes a jaunt with Olmstead.
We march past children seated in a scarlet wagon,
past the crimson roses of a wedding party,
the bride a speck of white among so much black.

We walk like ducks, pecking at notebooks,
strolling, a calligraphic caterpillar,
sampling scenery.

Near the lake's curves caressed by gold and maroon,
the crooked line meanders by a bench, its wood
silvery beneath new scratches. Up ahead,
a hillside awash in fresh-cut-grass-breeze

fingers pines, loosening cones
that land in lace knit by needles of ochre.
Acorns crunch underfoot in the meadow
where an oak of great age leans,

slicing the gunmetal sky
with cinereous precision
and from its crown
one bare branch
points the way.

Poets of a Certain Age Meet at Sara's

On this gray Saturday in winter, the poets marvel
at the curved stairwell walls and marble treads
leading to Sarah's third-floor old-mansion aerie.

After eating soup filled with spinach and beans,
they sit in a tight circle. Judy reads a bawdy ballad,
followed by serious, post nine-eleven fixation.

Sara's stinky sweater poem is a lesson in sestina.
Elaine's bad grocer-man revisions are lauded;
Helen opens an encyclopedia, studies

the escapades of Queen Elizabeth I.
Sara's two cats, one nice and one haughty,
skulk about, watch brown birds land

on the porch rail where snowflakes swirl
across skeletons of last summer's potted plants.
Inside, a vine wanders from window to window,

strays around a ceiling fixture.
Over goblets of cucumber water,
the poets learn that Joan's surgeon's wife

leaves traces of gin, and tears, on the beach.
Carol reads about the poets themselves,
something about the shadow of a fox...

From hairless panda baby, Anne steers to sparrows
perched between blades on a prison razor wire.
Ann relays a shoving match between two ants.

The nice cat falls off the windowsill at that.

Winter Light

Seven poets gather on a late December afternoon.
Alice reports a fall in the bathtub last week.

Joanne and Lyn lean on canes. Carol sports a titanium hip.
Juliana's vision dims. Harriet has become mute,

her mind gone rogue. Joyce feels invisible
in the grocery store; all nod in agreement,

each feeling the sting of age-related disappearance.
Yet the poems reveal selves without disability,

selves without disability or disguise--
the next life considered, what full-bodied contact

used to feel like. How winter light might be captured,
a light as elusive as youth. Someone strikes a match,

lighting a candle against the gathering dusk. Stanzas
flicker and flare, driving shadows into corners,

as if ink on paper, words themselves,
serve as beacons, brilliant in a starless night.

Where the Weasel Lurks

Shadowless Days

Last week:

cooler with rain
a little rain
a couple of showers
mostly clear with a shower
considerable cloudiness
showers possible
rather cloudy

This week:

today will be the first day
the sun will be seen all day
in over forty days

Next week:

cooler with rain
a little rain
a couple of showers
mostly clear with a shower
considerable cloudiness
showers possible
rather cloudy

February 13th

It's ten P.M.
and a knot of men
are gathered at the local drugstore
in the valentine section
of the greeting card aisle,
a six-foot-wide
slope of sentiment--
pilgrims in a trance
come to worshipbefore a pyramid,
faces serious,
foreheads glistening--
red velvet boxes and teddy bears
sprouting from under armpits
like misplaced organs--
and they reach over each
other's shoulders in pursuit
of the perfect verse,
the key that will open
temple doors
tomorrow night.

Anthophobia
The Fear of Flowers

I hear snowdrops whisper behind their hoods.
Pansies glare back. Daffodils stiffen, snicker;
peonies, pink, slander their white brethren.
Poison ivy creeps in. Day lilies will spend
twelve hours in gossip, roses will clamber

over the fence's hip, heliotrope will label
the fushia purple, ageratums taunt geraniums.
Soon, the black-eyed susan accuses
the begonia of being tuberous,
impatiens calls the nasturtium nasty.

What protection the trowel?
What good the spade?
I wear earplugs and gloves,
hide in the house,
tending to fake blooms.

But is that a murmur?
Did the silk rose belittle
the plastic lilac?
Maybe I should move.
To Antarctica.

But the flowering
hair grass,
the pearlwort…

Garden in Early Morning Light

Coneflowers wobble under the weight
    of bees, and heavy phlox heads nod.
    I spy dewdrops in day lily one-day throats.
    I observe, tend, prune.

But wait, what is this?
    Hordes have sprouted and spread--
    dandelions, nutsedge, and quackgrass,
    crab grass, its green legs spread wide.

Trowel, shovel, and hoe,
    two-tongued digger, weed-wacker,
    pitchfork and tiller, don't fail me now!
    I slash, chop, dig, burn.

This, and the odor of mulch
    and manure. One would think
    the effort too much, but for the feel
    of sweat dripping-- me,
    soaking into earth.

Trowel

Blister-giver
opener of sod,

you dull and pitted
hole-maker,

I can taste your aluminum
clasp on my tongue.

Oh, bulb-befriending
foe of weeds,

earthworm-dicer,
you deliver death.

Trowel, my season's hoof--
together we paw the garden,

transforming earth,
one scoop at a time.

Perfection

The ornamental turns a golden yellow
in late October, a huge fireball,
a comet anchored to our lawn.

"Maybe it's a fern-leaf European beech,
possibly a *fugus sylvatica asplenfloria*,"
says the nurseryman, "Don't disturb its roots."

Last summer, a laborer on a ladder
wielding a heavy power trimmer
sheared it into a flawless globe.

But brown leaves clinging to inner branches
hid a nest of eastern yellow jackets
full of zzzzzzzs--

and not even King Tut's dagger
of meteorite iron could protect him
from the fury of a thousand tiny darts.

Erythrophobia
Fear of the color red

I'm gonna
give up red

bye, bye
red meat
red skin potatoes
red snapper
and red
herrings, too

no more
blushing

cross off
red flags
red clover
redwoods
scarlet letters
not to mention
the Red Sea

forget
that redhead--
make *me*
your red hot
mama

I'm gonna keep
red blood cells
the Red Cross
and red wine...
which I might
need

Morning Show

A woman in short-shorts
teeters on patent-leather heels.
She tosses bleached tresses,
guides the talk show host

through a mansion-in-the-making.
Eleven bedrooms and thirteen bathrooms,
more square feet than the White House.
Her manicured nails trace along marble
countertops, imported from Spain.

She turns on solid gold faucets.
Somewhere between bedrooms
she becomes disoriented, lost,
in this unfinished shell,

and not even her impressive cleavage
can help navigate the way out--
she begins to laugh hysterically.
Cut to commercial.

If there is a heaven, this blonde
might find a special place reserved.
A crawl space.
Better yet, a mud-brick hut
without running water

Cognitive Dissonance

The multimillionaire owner of strip clubs
says his reputation has been ruined,
what with charges of prostitution
taking place in the curtained-off rooms
of his all-nude establishments.
He says his good name means everything,
plans to sell his ten-bedroom mansion,
go into the antique business.

At Thirty-Seven Hundred Feet

We pass over the final resting place
of the Titanic, slice between Lisbon
and Madrid, just as Clint Eastwood
develops macular degeneration,

loses his focus, and Shirley MacLaine
is discovered buried under potpies--
when I press the button to recline,
the seat does not budge. Algiers is below.

My headphones self-destruct, one ear
piece dangles, falls off. I get proficient
at lip-reading, consider Nigerian films.
At 600 miles per hour, my new blow-up

neck pillow fails to inflate, and there is no
toilet paper in economy class and someone
is throwing up.

Yes, the miracle of flight.

Cannibal

I ate Athens
swallowed
the Acropolis
whole

took tender forkfuls
of marble, white
and shining in the sun

tasted the temple
of Athena, licked
the stadium's shadow

I am becoming
a culture vulture

Key Lime Pie
Seeking that mid-Florida taste

We ate our way through
Western New York, one slice
at a time, letting our waistbands

out a notch, again and again--
"for science," you would say,
winking at me over the menu top.

This one, full of air, not tart
enough, that one, crust too thick.
Yet, regal in their whipped cream crowns,

wedge after wedge of translucent
gold-green was tasted - and buttons
continued to pop!

Here among home

improvement aisles,
I meditate at the altar
of paint chip paradise,

a mountain slope
of chromatic choice
in latex or oil.

Gray Expose
with an accent on the "e",
not even middle gray,

moss-kissed stone
or pale putty.
Its cranky neighbor,

Lead Cast, self-conscious
next to *Wetlands*,
no damp earth here,

more like gloom
crossed with pond scum.
but then there's *Croissant*,

yellowy as warm pastry
served by Hotel Du Lys.
Its neighbor, *Apricot Mousse*,

delicately blends golden
fruit and warm sun.
But then, my eyes taste

Cream Cake - vanilla bean
stirred into morning's light;
it melts my cones,

and stirs my taste buds, too.
But in the end, I leave
empty-handed, return home
to white walls.

A Full Buck Moon

The testosterone levels of American
men have been dropping since 1980

*Auster, barat, barber, blue norther,
churada, diablo, elephanta*

A study suggests that mobile phones
are causing wide-spread sperm damage

Gale, gust, hurricane, haboob, jet stream

Researchers are studying sexomonia,
a condition when people have sex while sleeping

Kubang, landlash, monsoon

Stimulating people's brains with electric current
while they sleep can improve memory

*Nor'easter, nor'wester, puelche,
quetzalcoatl, roaring forties*

Migratory birds practice alternating eye closure
permitting half the brain to sleep

*Sirocco. squall, tornado, twister,
typhoon, updraft, vortex*

The Himalayas are due for a mega earthquake
to drain a reservoir of seismic energy under Tibet

Willy-willy

Marsupial mothers who sleep around
give birth to bigger babies

Xlokk, yamo

Young male deer still sprout horns
in lockstep with the July moon

Zephyr

Stranger than Fiction

Deceit

A plastic dragonfly flutters
in the breeze, its wings fractioning
morning light into iridescence--

a real dragonfly alights on the fake one,
its yellow-striped body and wings
banded by tufts of black chenille.

I snap dozens of shots with my cell phone
but there is no clear resolution to be had;
no matter the setting, each one blurry,

and I am reminded of how desire distorts.
How a shadow is only a shadow.

How infatuation can change a chip of glass
caught in a sidewalk crack into a diamond.

Song of the Perseids

She devoured National Geographic
in the dentist's office, articles about star
nurseries, black holes, rings of gas.

But no glossy, full-color photo
could account for what she had seen.
Awakening in the middle of one deep

summer night, she knelt at the bottom
of her bed and peered up into the heavens.
Stars were dropping!

She rubbed her eyes, looked again.
Yes, tumbling by the handfuls!
She lay frozen under the weight

of being the only one to witness
the sky as it was falling.
A grown woman, she reads

that a grain of matter moving
at fifteen miles per second
becomes a shooting star,

that tons per day hit earth.
Yet she marks her calendar
for the next occurrence,

stays up all night, only
to find clouds hiding
the best sighting in years.

Boa Constrictor

One day, the boy woke to find
the family pet wrapped about his neck
after which the father threatened,
and the snake, sensing danger,
squeezed through a heating duct
into the wall.

No babysitter would sit after that.
No friends would visit.
The parents, frantic, called the zoo.
The zoo called the science museum.
How to coax a wayward mass
of muscle out of its labyrinth?

Finally, the mother, a practical woman,
bought a sturdy metal birdcage.
She bought a gerbil for the cage.

A day later, a man from Lockport
with tattoos and no teeth answered the ad.
Said he had a room for snakes,
spent hours unwrapping the snake
from the birdcage.

The gerbil went to live at a school
in a proper cage, faces pressed around,
where it twitched, it jumped
and promptly died from nerves.

Reflection in Three Parts
On Burchfield's "Dandelion Seed Heads and the Moon"

Above

In the quiet of the East gallery,
a jealous maiden rises full and white;
she shrieks, spills sheets of light,
blinding light, which shimmers
and stirs. Trees tilt. Crows grow silent.

Dragonflies dart in from the edges,
fresh from feeding they flutter,
storm-tattered. He calls,
she turns, opens her wings.

Below

Dandelion seed heads larger
than the moon and closer
echo the big head above,
their bright centers outshining hers.
A perilous equilibrium.

Tethers loosen,
tender parachutes open.
A few seeds pause above the seam
marking separation between earth and sky.
They hover, wait for the humid gust,
wait for the release, for the wandering--
time encased in brown eggs.

To One Side

The journals are stacked
slightly askew, the artist's life
deposited in sedimentary layers,
his handwriting even and legible--
Dead Sea Scrolls from West Seneca.

On the Wall

Sealed in reliquary frame,
an oak leaf the color of old leather
or ancient flesh, stands at attention
as if caught upright casting its shadow
across the grass of the neighboring yard,
a banner for a dying man in the dying light.

Café Exposé

He's in the usual spot,
computer before him,
like a shield. His fingers
play the keyboard,
while outside, sleet drives
sideways down Main Street.
Overhead, there's no snow
on the flat-faced television
tuned to the Food Channel,
sound turned off.

He's not bad looking,
could use new shoes.
He's eating something brown
with coffee, black.
He knows secrets--
tables are close,
chair backs touch,
an indiscretion revealed
during a lull in the hiss
of the espresso machine,
as the click of keys
pauses for a moment...

he's shaved his head,
grown a beard. He must think
no one will recognize him,
although he's as readable
as the newspaper
strewn across the counter.
He fears being home alone,
becoming the subject
of a short article on page nine,

"Man In Chair Was Dead For a Year…
found with television still playing."
Today, he's writing an editorial
about upscale coffee shops,
or he's a day-trader,
or worse, he's the Café Killer,
a snake biding his time.

At this, he glances over--
There's that woman again.
She sits by herself
in the same corner. Scratches
things down in a notebook.
Digs in her purse for another pen.
She always runs out of ink.
At last she shakes the pen,
scribbles on her sole.
Looks intense. Like a journalist
or college professor.
Maybe just a nutcase poet.
She's eating something beige
with her soy latté, decaf.
She's cut her hair,
makes her look younger.
Her glasses are new.
She knows secrets…

Shostakovich and Outer Space
Reverie during String Quartet No. 8 in C minor, op 110

I.

Horsetail hairs slither across strings,
largo announcing the snake as it encircles
a tree, knowing, even then, how this will end,
why light years separate humans from others.

II.

When the composer heard this work performed,
he buried his head in his hands and wept;
musicians left quietly, not knowing if politics,
illness, or his own hand would soon end Dimitri's life.

III.

Soon, a satellite will be released to record names
and addresses in solar neighbohoods, its wings
opening, like in this music, with a whir of allegretto
as life forms everywhere shiver, skitter into burrows
on unlit sides, and the persistence of radio signals
whips the horse that wanders lonely pastures at the edge,
and the reptile will hitch a ride to these other worlds.
The snake knows we cannot resist writing our own epitaphs
or biting into whatever we touch.

Pluto

Hubble sees

Pluto changing:

yellow-orange, molasses,

  to more crimson--

    alarming astronomers

      who forget their own

        decree: demotion

          from celestial nine

            to dwarf--

              even a tiny planet

                has feelings,

                  red rising

                    in round cheeks.

Concert in the Garden

The bass trombone player
cups the mute in his left hand,
flaps it up and down quickly,
slowly, a black rubber eyelid
opening and closing
in a golden throat.

The instrument sways,
becomes an insect's bow
birthing creature sounds,
courtship, preening--
quacks, squeaks, growls,
bleats, howls, clucks,
buzzes, chirps--
pachyderm to cricket,
an all-beast symphony.

And we're eavesdropping
in the garden; we're spying
on the horn man, getting down
on his knees, blowing
breath into mud.

A crack

appears in a massive window
so hairline that no one notices
until one day, it is longer.
Workmen come with ladders,
smooth tape upon the fracture,
as if paper and glue could be
a match for such forces.

That night, March wind blows,
or the building shifts, or glass
surrenders, shatters, pitches
a large slice of itself down;
half-inch thick tiles of smoky
brown scatter across concrete
in Andy Goldsworthy fashion.

I chance upon this scene--
brick walls framing morning light
streaming through the hole
high above, glancing off shards,
sparkling and dancing
in the interior gloom.
I stand transfixed behind tape
that cordons off the corner
like some crime scene,
more like a velvet
rope in a museum.

I return an hour later, camera
in hand, to document how a building
created its own art.
Not a sliver remains.
Why am I disappointed?

Broken glass. Nothing really.
Art, by accident? An act of physics?
Yet, a small, fleeting miracle--
sharp, fierce, inexplicable.

Lemon and Egg
On Artwork by Donald K. Sultan

   Imagine two
  thunderclaps. A pair
of lampblack belches from
a volcano's mouth. Smoke signals
pressed to the page in smudged
  syncopation, stacked upon each other
   and stuffed against the matt's edge,
     velveted by charcoal whose pressure
       furrows the paper. Light catches
         in these troughs. They look like
           plowed fields...but still,
               why the lemon, which
                  the egg?
            Balanced.
        It must be sorcery,
    sonic simile to tremolo and bombast,
   to bandoneon and timpani, all spit and spray
  around the edge, like sunspots erupting,
  black holes pulsing or a snowman's body stacked
 from coal and an already sizzling sort of alchemy.
The reflection in the glass quavers and I see myself,
stark against basalt darkness, ghostly. A shaky
version of me, an older self. And for a moment,
  I can scarcely remember who I am. Is this a trick?
  Or had the artist simply fallen down the chicken
    coop stairs one day with his pants pockets
      full of eggs, and he was pissed? Scrawled
       up the opposing side, his signature,
        once yolk yellow, has faded as
           marker pigments do.
                Memories, too.

Sciophobia Sciaphobia
The Fear of Shadows

Monet knew shadows
were mostly blue,
never black.
Haystacks aside,
mine are more dark,
stalking me, tracking
every move.
Stealthy, it climbs walls,
spreads over sidewalks,
grows or shrinks, always
a ghastly distortion.
I become a mere
silhouette, thin, obscure
or fat and indistinct,
or an outline on x-ray
blocked by an imaginary
malignant tumor mass,
an imitation me.
The sun conspires
in this daily charade
except when directly
overhead; cloudy days
and fog are my friends.
Even then, I do not have
a shadow of doubt
that my unwelcome
phantom-companion
lurks, lies in wait,
clutching the soles
of my shoes, salivating.

Ashokin Farewell

Pews are full. Doctors, lawyers, colleagues,
friends. They whisper among themselves,
note *how well she is holding up.*

She is dressed in black, hair styled, nails painted rose,
her appearance as put together as the church's interior,
whose apse's gold stars, under her direction,
have been applied by hand. Then, carefully chosen music--

the soprano, a granddaughter in her eighth month,
has agreed to sing, says later she had problems
with breath control. The pianist fingers Chopin,
although mourners observe his shoulders heave.

But it is not until her niece begins to bow the requested
"Ashokin Farewell" with its mournful, minor keys,
that the room blurs. She begins to shake. Shudder. Sob.
Her husband arises like a ghost behind her eyelids.

The buzzing in her ears overwhelms the chorus
of throat-clearing and then the low notes of the pipe,
pipe organ, pipe organ notes rise up through the soles
of her feet, pulling
                        her
                                    down.

Still Life in Egg Tempera

Low sun slips through blinds,
stripes Gina's fingers as she cracks
a fresh egg, separates the yolk.
Next to her easel, the morning paper
folds back to a black and white image,
"Iraqi Child Killed in Bombing."

The sun blazes down,
down on Akhtar, a scarf
wound round her head.
Her eyelashes are caked
with dust, eyes dark and dry.
Her fingers clutch rough wood.

Gina dries the gold yolk.
Slits it with a knife, coaxes
its liquid into a glass jar.
She pours distilled water,
stirs to a thin cream,
selects packets of pigments;
yellow ochre, raw sienna,
burnt umber.

Resting her head
on a rude box,
Akhtar mourns her only son.
His splintered nine years.
The lid warped, gapes,
a corner missing.

Gina mixes the color of pine,
of sand, of the howling wind.
She places an empty bird's nest
in the open mouth of a bowl

cupped by raven wings,
raises her brush to catch
the stream of light warming
the eggshell wall, thinner
than a child's skull.

Bridge

I point to the Arno,
so coffee-hued
that ducks float
undetected.
Gesture towards
the Ponte Vecchio
with its crown
of mud-colored shops
in whose windows
gold glints.

Tomorrow,
I will stand
in a long line
at the Uffizi,
climb steeply angled stairs
under a pimply
security guard's glare
to behold Venus
on her clam shell,
larger than imagined
and brighter

and gape
at the Duke of Urbino.
His small portrait
panel barely contains
the damaged nose,
the wiry black hair.

He adored his second
wife, the Duchess,
who is painted pallid,
a posthumous shadow.
They gaze at each other
across centuries
through oil-glazed eyes.

Nineteen Men
Yarnell Hill Fire, Arizona

Memorial Service: *July 9, 2013*

A caravan of nineteen hearses traverses
      the one hundred-twenty miles
      between Phoenix and Granite.
      Firefighters, police, and citizens
      line roads, salute the incinerated.
      Bars on Whiskey Row grow quiet

A red and white DC-3 flies overhead, casts
      its shadow across a makeshift memorial
      of water bottles, shovels and toy fire trucks
      placed by hands of children,
      releases ribbons bearing nineteen names
      which tangle in treetops

Fire Itself: *June 28, 2013*

No spark in a leaf-basket,
      no concubine of Mars,
      I am the daughter of lightning--
      I choose my own tango partners.
      Oxygen is my favorite--
      watch me swirl my skirts

I am who I am.
      Some would call me a Fierce Beauty.
      Am I angry? No. Red-backed manzanita
      shrubs are gasoline on a stick.
      I never regret torching them
      nor growing higher and higher

Reporters:

Nineteen men lay down on the ground,
    pulled on foil-lined tarps,
    waited for the wind to change.
    Except flames pirouetted on their backs
    and glue binding layers of shield
    came apart at five hundred degrees

Granite Mountain Hotshots:

Even as we lay on the warming earth,
    we trusted the opened shields
    with their minutes of oxygen,
    enough for a passing firestorm,
    safe to three hundred degrees
    and waited for the roar to pass

Reporters:

Nineteen men, captains of barbecue grills,
    exchanged spatulas for chainsaws,
    traded hamburgers for shovels,
    became Granite Mountain *Hotshots*--
    only to be grilled
    at temperatures higher than coals

Brendan McDonough: *Only survivor*

We went when we were called:
    all twenty of us, living the dream,
    thriving on adrenaline. I moved vehicles
    away from flames, as ordered. I saw
    shelters deployed. I am a shadow,
    a living pillar of ash

Rozsypne
One Year Later

In the deep sunflower-field outback
of Eastern Ukraine, a living woman,

or the body of a woman--
Igor was not entirely sure--

came whistling down, fell through his roof.
She landed face down in his kitchen,

naked but for her string underwear.
Thirty-nine others flew down, too.

Butt first, their hands and arms pointing up
says Galina, who sits on a bench in the shade

eating an apricot, her fingers shaking slightly.
Some were buckled into blue seats

of Flight 17, Malaysia Airlines.
Some arrived amid a patter of shoes.

Others landed in a cabbage patch,
a plot planted with rhubarb, an orchard.

Along a rutted dirt road, bunches
of wildflowers are still tied to trees.

Most villagers avoid walking on ground
blemished by unholy hail.

Often, they stare up at the sky.

Maple Springs
Buffalo News, Monday, December 29, 2014

On the second day of Christmas,
the day of two turtle doves,
Wesley, an eighty-five-year-old widower,
father of seven,
dresses in plaid shirt and denim,
buttons his navy blue pea coat,
pulls on a matching knit cap
and with his son, Benjamin,
a retired paramedic,
strolls down the driveway
on their way to a family party.

The men talk and laugh,
turn left onto Bayview Road.
It is an unseasonably warm
and moonless night.

Their sixty-five-year-old neighbor,
a widow known for good works,
changes into a fuzzy red sweater,
draws a comb through graying hair.
She zips up her down-filled jacket
and places a still-warm, home-baked
pie on the front seat of her minivan.
She puts it into gear. Backs out.

She approaches the two men,
her friends, from behind, near the spot
where years before, her husband
was killed. Maybe the dessert slides.
Perhaps she is lost in thought, or
her cataracts have ripened rendering
on-coming lights dazzling.
It was six o'clock pm.

What Remains

The maple in front of their house,
its roots sunk between sidewalk and street,
stands barren since her husband's death.

Oh, how he had loved that tree,
burning a fiery red that last autumn.
She withdraws a few crimson leaves

from a book on the coffee table.
As she fingers them, they crumble,
scatter across the carpet.

She stares out the window at empty limbs,
longing to feel her husband's body against hers,
to forget the sight of him keeling over.

Now she is a dead tree herself. Hollow.
An old sequoia. Maybe a paper birch,
eaten by borers. Or the chestnut outside

Ann Frank's attic window,
falling despite an armature of steel.
Like herself, corseted against grief.

She is lost in a shadow forest,
refusing to call the city about cutting
this tree down, even after its branch

crushes the hood of her car.
After dark, she caresses the maple's flank.
Presses the trunk to herself. Whispers.

Compost

Still clad in hospital green,
the body of an old woman
is brought to a serene hillside
at Western Carolina University.

She is laid on a bed of wood chips.
More chips are heaped atop her,
moisture added. Microbial
activity starts the pile cooking,
temperatures reaching high levels.
One hundred-forty degrees.
(There should be no smell).

Months later, her body
yields three feet by three feet
of material, minus bones.
Nothing is wasted.
Bodies have nutrients,
the young researcher says,
countless farms across
the country already compost
dead livestock.

A Flickering

A Matter of Perspective

On weekdays,
I fly to school.
I ride the wind
leaving no trail.
I am not a DC7.

More like a swallow
skimming and swooping
above the bus
in which noses
press against glass.

I am not a cardinal,
not a hawk,
but a dishwater plain
kid, bespectacled;
not Pegasus,

just a broad-backed
percheron.
Someday, I will
mount the jet stream
in a Boeing 747.
I will soar.

Five A.M.

The full moon hangs
        outside my bedroom
                window, spilling

an oblong of light
        across the carpet.
                I test its depths

with my big toe.
        As I walk back and forth,
                the light shimmers and stirs.

In the morning
        damp footprints
                lead back to bed.

Every Friday During Lent

In a darkened kitchen, Mother lights white candles
places them on a wooden chair. The three of us gather,
sink to our knees *upright, no slouching* on the cold
linoleum floor. Sorrowful mysteries unfold, illuminated
by booklets, ample guides through misery and death--

The Agony in the Garden
I wish I were a Methodist

The Scourging at the Pillar
My knees are killing me

The Crowning With Thorns
Why is Dad reading in the next room

The Carrying of the Cross
My sister is driving me nuts

The Crucifixion
I cannot feel my legs anymore

Hail Marys drone on. Now, my sister pokes me.
Mother's eyes are squeezed shut; she is transported.
I grasp each wooden rosary bead, mark time by how
many tiny globes remain. "Prayer is always the answer,"
Mother says. What do I know? For twenty plus years,
Church ladies prayed for the conversion of Russia
on rosaries of faceted red glass and sterling silver.
And we all know how that turned out.

A Bag of Cloth
After "A Jar of Buttons" by Ted Kooser

A cylinder stuffed with fabrics,
wrapped and pinned scraps

saved from stitching skirts and dresses
polka-dots, stripes, florals,

cottons, linens and wools
packed together in a long cloth

laundry tube, a core sample
of hand-sewn outfits in which I set forth

with the ancient Singer humming
leaving friends and family behind

years later my father burned this bag
in a cleaning fit, set fire to it in a metal can

out behind the apple orchard
never asking if it was stored in the closet

for a reason the quilt of my life
wafting upwards in paisley smoke

Regret

As the sun begins its dive,
I pull skinned-sapling bars
back through laddered gate,
drive heifers across the road.

The cows amble to the barn,
lured to milking by promise
of corn in their mangers.
But I do not follow.

I slide down the pond's bank,
parting cattails to lunge at frogs
who cower under lily pads.
I brush at flies, swat mosquitos.

At dusk, I head home, covered
in bites and pond scum.
Dinner over, I rifle through cupboards,
find cornbread crumbs on the stove.

Remorse shadows me years later,
as the memory of the dent I put
in biodiversity covers me thicker
than welts or algae ever could.

Agnes Agnes

Both my middle
names are the same.
Agnes, twice.

Whom to honor?
Agnes, shy aunt,
drowned at twenty-one.
Agnes, pinched
paternal grandmother,

or Agnes, martyr,
patron saint of virgins
and gardeners
Or maybe it was
the other Saint Agnes,
old-master-painted
with both breasts
cut off.

Oh. That was Agatha.

Even so, there should
be a painting of a woman
holding a plate upon which
quivers a single breast.
Whatever her name,
call her *my* patron saint.

Paint it triumphant.

Self-Portrait As One-Third Acre

The hedges and borders are still home
to rabbits, skunks, and something furry
that over-winters in the garage,
but the clump birch, borer-laden, is gone,
as are cherry trees that once lined the fence.
The crabapple, although pruned and fed,
is dressed in its last, fading cloud of pink.

Stunted on one side by silver maples
planted too close between road and lawn,
the Chinese elm arches lopsided,
its branches in jackets of gray-green fungus.
The ash's trunk, storm-split, sprouts shoots,
and the damaged horse chestnut flaunts
cones of white candles on misshapen candelabras.

The Japanese maple planted last fall endured
gales, freeze, and heave of bitter winter.
One branchlet succumbed, its stub hidden
under delicate spray of seven-fingered lace,
another reminder that this land's lineage
can be traced through survival, despite wounds
and imperfections, like a twisted spine,
lame hip, scars etched from clavicle to calf.

Suppose

Suppose the lump had not been cancer

Suppose that I never had learned to write poetry

Suppose that I had become a studio potter

Suppose that my father had gone to college

Suppose that my sister had not been overweight

Suppose that my mother's leukemia had not been acute

Suppose that I had arrived before she passed into unconsciousness

Suppose that I had not left the hospital just before my husband died

Cobblestones
Tepoztlan, Mexico

Kneeling among mounds of cobblestones,
workmen wield mallets, consider each rock.
    When one is found flawed or misshapen, it's set aside.
        If suitable, then tapped into place. Rhythms rise,
            like jazz...*tap,* ***tap****, tap, tap.*

I mark the road's daily progress. Camera clicking,
my shadow cast beside the men, I listen to their banter,
    their clack of tongue. They nod, smile.

At festival, a few days from now, one of them
arrayed in the full-body costume of the bull
    will charge me, his horned headdress lowered
        as it spins and spits fireworks. Again.
           And again.

Women will laugh as I shriek and run,
even those from whom I buy an egg and bolillo
    at market each morning. I will trip over my feet,
        drop my camera, pretend to grin.

        The next day, I pick up a pebble,
            slip it into my pocket.

The Calling

In the bottom drawer
of my nightstand,
I keep a box
of funeral cards,
some with Jesus
holding a lamb,
some, Mary hovering
over a half-moon
and the address of the deceased,
cemetery and plot,
imprinted on the back.
A few cards flaunt gold edges.
Others are laminated
to last for eternity.
Every so often, I finger
through the cards--
Aunt Frances,
a familiar fragrance,
Uncle Floyd,
a remembered turn of the head,
John from next door,
the rasp of a voice--
I piece together each person
but no matter how tenderly
I sniff the air
for Tabu or Old Spice,
mold atoms into
Uncle Floyd's face,
or listen for the cadence
of John's laughter,
I miss something--
yet if I stop remembering
they will cease to be.
It is my duty
to call them back.

Annual Visit to Evergreen Cemetery

My sister, squinting through the opaque mist,
points out hosta stems strewn on our parents' gravesite,
says they must have been weed-whacked. I suspect
that it was more likely a deer feeding frenzy,
but then, she and I disagree on almost everything.

Like who lived in the house at the bottom
of this cemetery's slope before arsenic, mercury,
and lead leaching downhill contaminated its well water.
Whether the girl in white who dances atop
its wrought-iron fence on full-moon nights is a legend.

Among slabs partially obscured by the relentless march
of lichen, are newer ones. For Ann, who never said her age,
her dates now permanent in granite. For my sister's boyfriend,
killed in Vietnam on his second day. Or the second week?
Oscar, who took his life with a bullet, or was it with rope?

During childhood, we came here in winter, threading
our way between tombstones to lay pine boughs on graves.
Grandmother's carved maiden name was the same as grandpa's.
Could they be first cousins? In spring, lilacs. Or peonies?
Definitely geraniums in July.

We visit less frequently now, strolling slowly along the lane
that weaves through this sacred space, our feet upon ruts
worn by wheels of horse-dawn carriages and now by automobiles
whose underbellies scrape against the hump between the two.
We follow parallel tracks.

The Night My Sister's House Burned Down

Six o'clock. I am sitting at a stop sign
waiting for traffic to clear and shaking
my head in disbelief.

Heat building up in the wall behind
a woodstove is producing tongues that lick
pre-Civil War lath, a blaze that refuses

to leave shadow-scorches upon plaster,
instead whirling beds, dressers, chairs
into evenly strewn ash.

I see them from two hundred miles away,
flames dancing above the tree line,
leaping and orange.

The phone call comes at midnight.
I already know it happened at six o'clock,
how tall the flames, how dark the night...

Passage

Mars was closer to earth that evening
than it had been in sixty thousand years.
Tethered to twin oxygen tanks,
you struggled up from the chair,
shuffled across the living room,
navigated the dining room's
wrinkled rug ravines,
crossed through the kitchen,
out the heel-biting door,
down two steep steps,
over winter-heaved bricks
to the edge of the patio--
you, an earthbound astronaut
awestruck at the sight
of the red orb hanging low overhead--
but all I saw were the tumors
in your lungs, how on the x-rays
they looked like pinpoints of light,
like constellations in a black night,
like planets way too close.

The Visit

Last night, my dead husband
appeared at the front door
dressed in a new suit,
a fresh sunflower tattoo
poking its head
from under his shirt collar.

It seemed natural
that we go out to eat.
While waiting for a table,
I sewed the underarm
splits in my dress's seams
with raffia offered by a child.

Her blonde hair swirled
and dinner was delayed--
the inn full
of prosperous Presbyterians
who drank too much,

bursting into hymns
that sounded angelic.
I awoke with a feeling
of fullness, prick marks
on my middle fingertip,

like the memory of the child
we never had, a girl
whose face followed
the light.

The Yearning

Bluestem

This ache is the yearning that greens
        the bulb buried deep in earth. It fingers

its way toward the sun. No,
        this ache is the urge of an old log

under the thrall of summer rain
        to sprout an extravagance of mushrooms. No,

in each other's arms, we dance, two moths
        twirling on moonbeams, pheromones calling

body to body. Oh, yes, this ache is the fire
        frenzy. Like prairie grass courted by lightning,

I scatter...

Petrichor
The smell that arises when rain falls on dry earth

"Let's take a walk," you said,
but now raindrops run down our faces,
a few at first, then rivulets that plaster
hair to heads, leaving only cowlicks standing.
Water squishes between sneakered toes
as we laugh and sprint back to my house.
Inside, I toss you a towel, try not to look
while you strip off your shirt, exchange it
for a crumpled one that you fished out
from under your car seat. And I hope
that you do not notice how mascara
is running down my cheeks
or that with the smell of you,
breath catches in my throat--
I want to press you to me, iron out
wrinkles with the steam heat
of our bodies and kiss until
we are each other's shelter
for all storms to come.

Unrequited Love

The cemetery is near
a young fig tree,
whose fruit is like a lemon,
so bitter, like your heart.

I call up your voice,
less painful if it had been
a frozen orange
caught in my throat.

Love ascended between us--
but who loves enough?
He who loves attracts fruit flies.

Round

She finds herself awake at midnight,
drawn by light of the full moon spread
across the floor like gossamer

and she wants to wrap herself in it,
not as in a shroud, but more like a sugar
cookie layered under cellophane.

Groping for a bedside pen, she scribbles
in the tattered notebook, struggles to capture
this and other thoughts before they slip

through her fingers like shadows do.
She is careful not to disturb her husband
whose bald head on the pillow shines--

but he stirs, turns, and wraps his arm
about her, cupping her breast in his hand,
its nipple as pale as the moon.

Passion

Let me spread poems
one by one over you,
wrapping you in my words
so that our sweat releases
ink from the page,
like midnight blue sap,
and it sinks into your pores
indelibly staining you
with me.

Special Thanks

To the Lake Erie Poets, Ann, Anne, Elaine, Jennifer, Joan, Judy and Noreen for their support, for the poetry workshops taken at the Chautauqua Writers Center, to Marge Norris for introducing me to the world of poetry, to Ann Goldsmith for her keen editor's eye, to ryki zuckerman who has assisted greatly in getting my poems out into the public, to my publisher, Len Kagelmacher, to the late Thomas Sist who encouraged me to write in the first place, and to my beloved husband, John, for his patience and enthusiasm.

About the Poet

Photo by Nick Butler

Carol Townsend received her BS in Art from Nazareth College of Rochester and her BFA in Applied Design in Ceramics from Ohio University. She is an Associate Professor of Art and Design and former Chair of the Design Department at the State University College of New York at Buffalo. As an award winning ceramicist and mixed media artist, her works are represented in numerous collections. She has been a frequent participant in the Chautauqua Writers' Center poetry workshops and has served on the board of the Chautauqua Literary Arts Friends. One of her poems was first runner up in the 2019 National Carolyn Forche Prize competition sponsored by Waterwood Press.

Her poems have appeared in the journals *Voices de la Luna* and *Sow's Ear*, in *The Buffalo News*, and on the *Master Poetry Ink* website. She has been an invited reader in the *Gray Hair*, *Rooftop*, *Wordflight*, *Red Door* and *Literary Cafe Series* in Buffalo, New York. Her first chapbook, *A Cinder In My Knee*, was published by Buffalo Arts Publishing in 2016.

An avid gardener and photographer, she resides with her husband, John, and dachshund, Max, in Snyder, New York.

www.ingramcontent.com/pod-product-compliance
Lightning Source LLC
Chambersburg PA
CBHW041313110526
44591CB00022B/2899